SCOTLAND

YOUR ULTIMATE TRAVEL GUIDE TO EXPLORING SCOTLAND

Walter Boat

All rights reserved. No part of this publication may be reproduced, distributed, or transmitted in any form or by any means, including photocopying, recording, or other electronic or mechanical methods, without the prior written permission of the publisher, except in the case of brief quotations embodied in critical reviews and certain other noncommercial uses permitted by copyright law.

TABLE OF CONTENTS

INTRODUCTION TO SCOTLAND 7

CHAPTER 1 11

  Planning Your Trip to Scotland 11

  When to Go 13

    Summer (June-August) 13

    Autumn (September-November) 14

    Winter (December-February) 14

    Spring (March-May) 15

  How to Get There 18

    By Airplane 18

    By Train 18

    By Bus 19

    By Car 19

    By Ferry 20

  Where to Stay 22

    Edinburgh 23

    Glasgow 24

    The Highlands 24

    Isle of Skye 25

    Inverness 26

    Aberdeenshire 27

    The Outer Hebrides 27

    Orkney Islands 28

CHAPTER 2 .... **30**
  Must-See Attractions in Scotland 30
    The Edinburgh Castle 30
    Loch Ness 32
    Isle of Skye 35
    Stirling Castle 37
    The Royal Mile 40
    Kelvingrove Art Center and Museum in Glasgow 43
    The Scottish Highlands 45
    The Cairngorms National Park 48

CHAPTER 3 .... **52**
  Experiencing Scotland's Culture 52
    Music and Sounds 54
    Meals and beverages 58
    Shopping and Crafts 63

CHAPTER 4 .... **68**
  Exploring Scotland's Natural Beauty 68
    Hiking and Walking 71
    Wildlife and Nature 75
    Water Activities 78
  Conclusion 83

INTRODUCTION TO SCOTLAND

Sarah hopped on the flight to Scotland on a cool summer morning. She had only ever imagined going to the nation she had heard so much about, and now she would have the opportunity.

Sarah experienced a wave of emotion as the aircraft descended. She had a strong sense of belonging in Scotland, as if her spirit had been there all along. She couldn't believe she had arrived at this point.

The locals greeted Sarah warmly as she stepped off the plane and appeared to identify her as an American. They were welcoming and helpful, which only enhanced Sarah's good time. Over the course of her visit, Sarah explored the country's many attractions, from the ancient castles to the stunning lochs. Everywhere she went, she was met with a friendly smile and a warm welcome.

During her trip, Sarah fell in love with Scotland and knew she had to return. She started organizing her move because she was resolved to make this her home.

Two years later, Sarah had successfully settled down and was happy to call Scotland her home. She adored everything about her new place, including the residents and the surroundings. She frequently passed her days wandering the countryside and appreciating its grandeur.

Sarah had fallen in love with Scotland and couldn't imagine residing anywhere else. Now that she had found her new home, she was resolved to make the most of it.

Years later, Sarah is still filled with nostalgia for the day she first set foot in Scotland. She will never forget how happy she was to be welcomed by the populace and how she felt the nation had become her home.

Sarah will continue to travel to Scotland for years to come because it will always hold a special spot in her heart.

The best vacation resource for Scotland is here! Scotland is a nation full of breathtaking natural beauty and a rich cultural heritage, from the rolling hills of the Highlands to the rugged coastlines of the islands. You can use the knowledge in this guide to make the ideal Scotland travel arrangements.

Along with comprehensive information on the nation's main cities and regions, you'll also find hints and pointers on the best locations to go, things to do, places to eat, and places to stay. Along with learning about regional norms and etiquette, you'll also learn about Scotland's history, culture, and traditions.

This guide will help you make the most of your journey, whether you're searching for a tranquil retreat or an exciting adventure. Scotland has something for everyone, from the vibrant towns of Glasgow and Edinburgh to the isolated Highland villages. So let's begin your incredible trip through Scotland!

Scotland is a place with something for everyone, from the untamed and uninhabited islands of the Outer Isles to the busy streets of Edinburgh. You will find all the information you require in this thorough handbook to help you create the ideal Scotland vacation. You can make the most of your time in Scotland by visiting the main cities and areas and learning about the history and culture of the nation.

You can discover comprehensive information on the top tourist destinations, enjoyable activities, and places to eat, drink, and stay. Additionally, you'll learn about the nation's traditions, manners, and must-see sights.

This guide will enable you to get the most out of your Scottish adventure, whether you're searching for a tranquil getaway or an action-packed vacation.

So, collect your passport and prepare to travel around Scotland. You can use the knowledge in this guide to make the ideal Scotland travel arrangements. Let's get going!

CHAPTER 1

Planning Your Trip to Scotland

Do you have travel to Scotland on your mind? Scotland is an incredibly attractive nation with a fascinating past, welcoming people, and a wide variety of things to see and do. Here are some suggestions to make the process of organizing your trip to Scotland as stress-free as possible. Planning a trip to Scotland can be thrilling and intimidating.

Determine the duration of your trip before anything else. Scotland is a vast and diverse nation, so it's crucial to schedule your time appropriately. If you are only in town for a brief while, you might want to concentrate on seeing the main attractions. If you have more leisure, you can travel further or look for more obscure locations. In either case, it is important to plan your days and make sure you are making the most of your time in Scotland.

Next, choose your destination. The various areas that make up Scotland each have their own distinct charm and culture.

The Highlands, Islands, and Borders regions provide breathtaking scenery and a wealth of possibilities for outdoor activities, and Edinburgh and Glasgow are both cities worth visiting. To make the most of your journey, do your research on the attractions, lodging, and transportation options in each region once you have chosen which ones you want to visit.

You have lots of choices when it comes to lodging. Every income can be accommodated, from luxury hotels to cheap hostels. Consider staying in an Airbnb or hostel if your travel money is limited. You can experience the sights and sounds of the city center because hostels are frequently located in the center of cities. Hotels typically cost more but come with more extras like eateries, spas, and swimming pools.

When organizing your journey to Scotland, transportation is a crucial factor. You might want to think about renting a vehicle if you plan to visit several places. You'll be able to travel further and take in more of the nation as a result.

You can also take advantage of public transportation, such as buses and trains, to get around.

Lastly, remember to account for the unforeseen.

Make careful to pack appropriately because Scotland's weather can be erratic. It's a good idea to carry a GPS or map with you so you can navigate. In case something unexpected occurs, be sure to have the contact information for your lodging and transportation.

You can maximize your journey to Scotland and guarantee a pleasurable and unforgettable experience by paying attention to these suggestions. Get out there and experience Scotland—there is a lot to see and do there!

When to Go

One of the most crucial choices you'll have to make when organizing a journey to Scotland is when to go. Due to Scotland's temperate maritime environment, the entire year is typically mild and rainy. However, there are some clear seasonal differences that can have a significant effect on your trip.

Summer (June-August)
Scotland's summer travel season is very popular, and for good cause. Temperatures typically range from 10-20°C (50-68°F) and are dry and pleasant.

Exploring the Scottish landscape and engaging in outdoor pursuits like hiking, cycling, and fishing are ideal at this time of year. Additionally, you can squeeze more into your day thanks to the lengthy daylight hours. However, keep in mind that during this time, prices for lodging and activities might increase, and popular tourist locations might become very crowded.

Autumn (September-November)

Scotland can be visited in the fall, when the tourist throngs from the summer have thinned out and the landscape is ablaze with vibrant foliage. Be ready for cooler weather because temperatures can vary from 5 to 15 °C (41 to 59 °F). The Braemar Gathering and the Royal National Mod are just a couple of the well-known events that can be enjoyed in Scotland during the months of September and October.

Winter (December-February)

Scotland's winter season is stunning, with snow-covered mountains and glistening frost-covered scenery. Be ready for the cold; temperatures can vary from -2 to 7 degrees Celsius (28 to 45 degrees Fahrenheit).

Skiing, snowboarding, and ice skating are just a few of the unique winter sports that can only be done in Scotland during the winter. Be conscious, though, that some lodgings and tourist attractions might be closed during the winter.

Spring (March-May)

Scotland can be visited in the spring, when the weather begins to warm up and the countryside begins to blossom. Be ready for cooler weather because temperatures can vary from 5 to 15 °C (41 to 59 °F). Glasgow's St. Patrick's Day celebrations are best experienced in March, and Edinburgh's renowned Beltane Fire Festival is best experienced in May.

Overall, your interests and tastes will determine the best time to visit Scotland. Summer is a great option if you're searching for drier conditions and outdoor activities. Autumn is the best season if you enjoy events and vibrant foliage.

Winter is the best season to enjoy snow-covered landscapes and winter activities. Spring is also the ideal season to visit if you want to see the countryside in bloom. Scotland will undoubtedly make a lasting impression on you, regardless of when you visit.

When choosing when to visit Scotland, there are a few additional factors to take into account in addition to the weather and seasonal activities. The quantity of daylight is one of the most crucial factors. Scotland is renowned for having lengthy summer days; in some locales, the length of the day in June can reach 17.

If you want to squeeze in as much sightseeing and outdoor activities as you can, this can be a huge benefit. The reverse may be true during the winter, when there are fewer daylight hours and very short days. Due to this, it may be difficult to squeeze everything you want to do into one day, so make sure to plan your schedule carefully.

The price of transport and lodging should also be taken into account. Since the summer is Scotland's busiest travel season, costs for travel, lodging, and events are frequently higher than they are at other times of the year.

If you're on a tight budget, you might want to think about going during the shoulder season (April through May or September through October), when costs are lower and throngs are smaller.

Last but not least, it's crucial to be conscious of any significant occasions or holidays that may be occurring while you're there. For instance, one of the biggest arts events in the world, the Edinburgh Festival Fringe in August, draws tourists from all over the world.

Although it can be a fantastic time to visit Edinburgh, it can also be very busy and crowded, with higher costs and less lodging availability. It's crucial to study any significant occasions or holidays that will fall during your trip and make appropriate plans.

In conclusion, the best time to visit Scotland will rely on a number of variables, such as the weather, seasonal activities, daylight hours, cost, and significant events. The ideal moment to travel will ultimately depend on your personal preferences and interests.

Scotland is a stunning and alluring location that is sure to make an impact on you, whether you're looking to explore the Scottish countryside, take part in distinctive festivals and events, or enjoy winter sports.

How to Get There

Travelers have a variety of choices for transportation, making it fairly simple to get to Scotland. Some of the most popular methods to travel to Scotland are listed below:

By Airplane

Scotland is home to a number of international airports, the biggest of which are Glasgow International Airport and Edinburgh Airport. Inverness Airport and Aberdeen International Airport are two more significant terminals.

Direct flights are offered from a large number of important cities around the globe to these airports by a variety of airlines. You can simply rent a car or use public transportation to get to your destination once you get there.

By Train

Scotland has a vast rail system that connects the nation's main cities and towns. ScotRail, the primary train company, provides frequent services to locations all over Scotland. Additionally, there are direct rail connections between London and Glasgow and Edinburgh. A train might be a practical and affordable choice if you're leaving from the UK.

By Bus

Several bus companies, including National Express and Megabus, provide routes to and from Scotland.

Both larger Scottish cities like Edinburgh and Glasgow as well as more rural towns and villages nationwide are served by these carriers.

If you're on a tight budget, taking the bus can be a good choice, but be aware that it may take longer than other forms of transportation to get where you're going.

By Car

Driving to Scotland is a great choice if you are coming from the UK or Europe. Driving can be a fantastic way to experience Scotland's beautiful countryside because the nation is well-connected by a network of motorways and main roads. If you're traveling by car from another part of Europe, you must first take a ferry to the United Kingdom before heading north to Scotland.

By Ferry

Because Scotland is an isolated country, a number of ferry companies provide services to and from Scotland. There are frequent services to the Orkney and Shetland Islands, and the major ferry ports are in Ullapool, Scrabster, and Aberdeen. If you're going from Northern Ireland or the Republic of Ireland, there are also ferry services to ports in Scotland.

Travelers have a variety of choices for transportation, making it fairly simple to get to Scotland. There are many ways to travel to Scotland and begin experiencing all that this lovely country has to offer, including flying, taking a train or bus, taking a car, or taking a ferry.

The most popular mode of transportation for Americans going to Scotland is by air. Many airlines provide direct flights to Edinburgh or Glasgow from significant U.S. locations like New York, Boston, and Chicago. Depending on the airline and your departure city, the journey lasts anywhere from 7 to 8 hours.

The season of the year you intend to journey should be taken into account when making your flight arrangements.

The summer months are Scotland's busiest travel times, so prices for tickets and lodging tend to be higher then. Traveling in the shoulder seasons (April–May or September–October) may be a good idea if you're on a tight budget because prices are typically cheaper and crowds are smaller.

There are several ways to get around Scotland once you get there. If you intend to remain in a city or a large town, there are many bus and train options that are both accessible and reasonably priced.

Renting a car is a wonderful option for people who want to explore rural or remote areas. Due to the narrow roads and driving on the opposing side of the road in Scotland, be aware that driving can be difficult.

Keep in mind that Scotland employs a different currency than the United States if you're an American traveler. The British pound serves as the official currency in Scotland, so you should swap your dollars for them before traveling there. Banks, airports, and currency exchange offices all offer currency exchange services, but be aware that exchange rates and fees can differ.

Last but not least, it's crucial to find out if you need a visa to visit Scotland if you're an American traveler. For brief vacation stays, Americans do not require a visa; however, if you intend to work or stay in Scotland for an extended length of time, you may need a visa. Check the prerequisites and submit your visa application well in advance of your journey.

In conclusion, air travel is the most popular method of transportation for Americans visiting Scotland. When making travel plans, it's essential to take into account the season, available modes of transportation, the exchange rate, and visa requirements. You can have a wonderful and unforgettable trip to Scotland with some advance planning and study.

Where to Stay

Scotland is a nation with a fascinating past, breathtaking natural scenery, and energetic cities. Choosing a place to remain can be challenging when there is so much to see and do. In Scotland, there are many choices for lodging, ranging from inexpensive hostels to opulent hotels and everything in between. In this tour, we'll look at some of Scotland's top lodging options and the amenities they have to offer.

Edinburgh

Scotland's capital, Edinburgh, is among the most well-liked travel locations in the world. The city is renowned for its magnificent building, exciting nightlife, and extensive cultural history.

Edinburgh offers a wide variety of lodging choices, from high-end hotels to inexpensive hostels.

There are several hostels in the city that provide clean, comfortable lodging at a reasonable price if you're searching for a low-cost option. The Castle Rock Hostel is a well-liked hostel that is close to Edinburgh Castle and provides breathtaking vistas of the city.

In Edinburgh, there are many high-end accommodations to choose from for a more opulent stay, including the five-star The Balmoral in the center of the city.

Glasgow

Scotland's biggest city, Glasgow, is a center for entertainment, history, and culture. The city offers a wide variety of lodging choices, including premium chains, boutique hotels, and hostels that are affordable.

If you're on a tight budget, Glasgow has a number of inexpensive dormitories that provide tidy and welcoming lodging.

The Euro Hostel Glasgow, which provides affordable rooms in the center of the city, is one well-liked choice.

Glasgow offers a wide selection of upscale lodging options, including the five-star Blythswood Square Hotel, which is housed in a landmark Georgian structure.

The Highlands

Scotland's vast and rugged Highlands region is home to breathtaking natural beauty, a feeling of seclusion, and tranquility. The Highlands are the ideal location to stay if you want to get away from the bustle of the city.

The Highlands offer a wide variety of lodging choices, from inviting bed and breakfasts to opulent lodges. Consider staying in a traditional Scottish castle, like the Dornoch Castle Hotel or the Eilean Donan Castle Hotel, if you're searching for a one-of-a-kind and unforgettable experience.

Isle of Skye

Off Scotland's west shore is the lovely and inaccessible Isle of Skye.

The island is well-known for its rocky terrain, historic castles, and conventional Scottish way of life.

The Isle of Skye offers a variety of lodging choices, including bed and breakfasts, guesthouses, and cabins with full kitchens. The Kinloch Lodge Hotel and Restaurant, a posh hotel housed in an old hunting lodge on the southern tip of the island, is one well-liked choice.

Saint Andrews

Scotland's east coast is home to the historic town of St. Andrews, which is renowned for its beautiful beaches, top-notch golf facilities, and deep-rooted culture.

The town offers a variety of lodging choices, from luxurious hotels to guesthouses that are affordable. One popular hotel in St. Andrews is the Old Course Hotel, a luxurious five-star hotel located right on the famous Old Course golf course. For a more budget-friendly option, consider staying at a guesthouse or bed and breakfast, such as the Dunvegan Guest House or the Five Pilmour Place Guest House.

Inverness

The biggest city in the Scottish Highlands, Inverness, is a well-liked vacation spot for people traveling to the area. The city is renowned for its breathtaking natural surroundings, lively culture, and extensive past.

Inverness offers a wide range of lodging choices, including motels, guesthouses, and hostels that are affordable.

The Rocpool Reserve Hotel and Chez Roux Restaurant, an opulent five-star hotel situated in the center of the city, is one well-liked lodging option. Consider staying at the Black Isle Hostel, a neat and cozy hostel housed in a historic structure in the heart of the city, for a more cost-effective choice.

Aberdeenshire

Northeastern Scotland's Aberdeenshire is a gorgeous area distinguished by its breathtaking coastline, charming fishing towns, and ancient castles.

From quaint bed and breakfasts to opulent motels, the area offers a variety of lodging choices.

The Trump International Golf Links and Hotel, an opulent five-star hotel with direct access to the shore and breathtaking views of the North Sea, is one of Aberdeenshire's most well-known lodging options. Consider staying at a bed and breakfast like the Ardenlea House Bed and Breakfast or the Ballater Hostel for a more affordable choice.

The Outer Hebrides

A group of islands off the shore of Scotland's west coast, the Outer Hebrides are renowned for their untamed beauty, illustrious past, and distinctive culture. The islands offer a variety of lodging choices, from inviting bed and breakfasts to opulent motels.

The Harris Hotel, a posh four-star hotel with breathtaking sea views on the island of Harris, is one of the most well-known accommodations in the Outer Hebrides.

Consider staying at a bed and breakfast like the Tigh Na Mara Bed and Breakfast or the Westview Bed and Breakfast for a more affordable choice.

Orkney Islands

A remote group of islands off Scotland's north shore, the Orkney Islands are renowned for their ancient history, breathtaking scenery, and distinctive culture. The islands offer a variety of lodging choices, from inviting bed and breakfasts to opulent motels.

The Kirkwall Hotel, a traditional Scottish hotel in the center of Kirkwall with breathtaking views of the nearby countryside, is one well-liked lodging option in the Orkney Islands. Consider staying at a bed and breakfast like the Avalon Guest House or the Karrawa Guest House for a more affordable choice.

In conclusion, Scotland offers a wide variety of lodging choices to suit all tastes and financial ranges. In Scotland, there is something for everyone, whether you're looking for an opulent hotel in the middle of a metropolis or a warm bed and breakfast in a remote area.

Consider your spending limit, ideal location, and the kind of experience you want when deciding where to remain.

CHAPTER 2

Must-See Attractions in Scotland

Scotland is a beautiful country with a rich past, culture, and natural beauty. There are many must-see attractions that bring visitors from all over the globe, ranging from ancient castles to breathtaking landscapes. This chapter will showcase some of the best attractions in Scotland that you should not miss.

The Edinburgh Castle
Edinburgh Castle is one of Scotland's most recognizable landmarks and a must-see for any tourist. The castle has a long history, going back over 1,000 years, and has served as a royal residence, military stronghold, and prison. Visitors can now tour the castle's many exhibits and admire the city from the castle's ramparts. Edinburgh Castle is one of the most iconic landmarks in Scotland, located at the top of Castle Rock in the heart of Edinburgh's Old Town. The castle has a rich and varied history that dates back over 1,000 years and has played a central role in many key moments in Scotland's history.

The Scottish Crown Jewels, also known as the Honours of Scotland, are one of the most famous attractions at Edinburgh Castle. The Honours are a crown, scepter, and sword from the 15th and 16th centuries that were used in the coronation of Scottish kings. Visitors can get a close look at these historic artifacts and learn about their importance in Scottish history.

The Great Hall, which was built by King James IV in the early 16th century, is another famous attraction at Edinburgh Castle. The hall is a stunning example of medieval building, with intricate carvings and heraldic insignia. Visitors can tour the hall and learn about its history while also admiring the city views from its windows.

Another highlight of Edinburgh Castle is the Royal Palace, which consists of a number of rooms once used by the Scottish monarchs for state ceremonies and formal business. Visitors can tour the palace's many exhibits, including the King's and Queen's bedchambers, the State Dining Room, and the Royal Apartments, which have been beautifully restored.

The National War Museum of Scotland is a must-see attraction at Edinburgh Castle for those interested in Scotland's military past. The museum exhibits weapons, uniforms, and artifacts from important battles and conflicts from the medieval era to the present day.

Finally, don't skip the views from Edinburgh Castle. Visitors can experience panoramic views of the city, including the renowned Edinburgh skyline, as well as the surrounding hills and countryside, from the castle's ramparts. Bring your camera and snap lots of pictures to remember your visit to this iconic Scottish landmark.

Loch Ness

Loch Ness is a big, deep freshwater loch in the Scottish Highlands best known for the Loch Ness Monster, its legendary resident. While the monster is the primary attraction for many visitors, the lake itself is a breathtaking natural wonder. Visitors can take lake boat excursions, explore the surrounding forests, and learn about the area's history and geology at the nearby Loch Ness Centre and Exhibition.

Loch Ness, situated in the Scottish Highlands, is one of the most renowned and mysterious bodies of water in the world. It is perhaps best known for the mythical Loch Ness Monster, or "Nessie" as it is fondly known.

Visitors to Loch Ness can experience the various activities and attractions the region has to offer. One of the most well-liked activities is having a boat tour of the loch, where you can discover the region's past and local legends while taking in the breathtaking scenery. Some trips even employ sonar technology to look for Nessie's footprints!

There are a lot of historical sites to visit in the area of Loch Ness for history buffs. One of the most well-known is Urquhart Castle, which is situated on the loch's edge and dates to the 13th century. The castle has been crucial to many significant events in Scottish history and served as a critical stronghold during the Scottish Wars of Independence. The abandoned fortress can be explored by visitors, who can also gaze out over the loch from its walls.

The Caledonian Canal, which connects Loch Ness with other nearby bodies of water through a number of locks and waterways, is another well-liked destination in the area.

It runs from Inverness to Fort William. Visitors can hire a canoe or kayak to explore the waterways at their own speed or take a leisurely boat ride along the canal.

The region around Loch Ness is a haven for hikers, cyclists, and environment lovers who enjoy outdoor activities. Along the length of the loch, on the Great Glen Way, a well-liked hiking path, are breathtaking vistas of the mountains and countryside. There are a lot of cycling paths nearby as well, from easy strolls to difficult mountain bike tracks.

Finally, a visit to the Loch Ness Centre and Exhibition is a must for any excursion to Loch Ness. The history and legends of Loch Ness, including the tale of Nessie and the numerous sightings and theories surrounding the creature, are examined in this museum and tourist center. The mysteries of Loch Ness are brought to life through interactive exhibits, movies, and displays for visitors to appreciate.

Overall, Lake Ness is a unique and stunning location that has something to offer everyone.

There are plenty of things to see and do in this famous Scottish location, whether you're interested in history, outdoor pursuits, or the Loch Ness Monster mythology.

Isle of Skye

The Isle of Skye has some of Scotland's most picturesque scenery, including a rocky shoreline, undulating hills, and towering peaks. The Old Man of Storr rock formation, the breathtakingly gorgeous Fairy Pools, and the historic Dunvegan Castle are just a few of the many attractions on the island that can be explored by tourists.

Off Scotland's west coast lies the gorgeous and untamed Isle of Skye, which is renowned for its stunning landscapes, rocky coastline, and extensive history and culture. The Isle of Skye is a must-see location for anyone visiting Scotland because of its abundance of natural and cultural draws.

The Cuillin Mountains, a striking collection of summits that dominate the island's skyline, are among the most well-known sights on the Isle of Skye. These mountains provide some of Scotland's finest hiking and climbing opportunities, with routes that range from easy strolls to strenuous multi-day treks.

The Quiraing, an area of rough cliffs, hills, and plateaus that is both breathtakingly gorgeous and uncannily otherworldly, is another well-liked attraction on the Isle of Skye. On foot, visitors can investigate this distinctive setting and take in the breathtaking views of the nearby landscape and the sea.

The Island of Skye has a lot to offer people who are interested in history and culture as well. One of the island's most well-known sights is Dunvegan Castle, which dates back more than 800 years and is still the MacLeod clan's residence.

The renowned Fairy Flag, a mysterious artifact thought to have the power to protect the MacLeod family, is one of the many rooms and displays that visitors can explore at the castle.

Many traditional Scottish towns and settlements, each with its own special charm and personality, can be found on the Isle of Skye. With its colorful houses lining the harbor and a variety of stores, eateries, and art galleries to discover, Portree is the island's largest town and a well-liked tourist location.

With centuries-old traditional buildings and design, other villages, like Dunvegan and Broadford, provide a glimpse into the island's rich history and culture.

The Isle of Skye is also a haven for adventure enthusiasts, offering countless chances for hiking, fishing, kayaking, and wildlife viewing. Off the coast, visitors can see dolphins, whales, and seals, and they can also hike through the island's many parks and nature areas to take in the breathtaking scenery and diverse wildlife.

Overall, anyone visiting Scotland should make sure to explore the Isle of Skye. The island has something to offer for everyone thanks to its breathtaking landscapes, rich history and culture, and abundance of outdoor activities and sites.

Stirling Castle

The Scottish city of Stirling is home to the ancient fortress known as Stirling Castle. This famous castle, which has served as a royal residence, a fortress, and a representation of Scottish freedom, has been significant in the history of the nation.

Stirling Castle's architecture, which combines aspects of both medieval and Renaissance design, is one of its most striking features.

The Great Hall of the palace is especially noteworthy because of its intricate wooden ceiling and fine carvings. The royal apartments, the kitchens, as well as the many courtyards and parks of the castle, are just a few of the numerous other rooms and attractions open to visitors.

The past of Stirling Castle is also extensive, going back more than 800 years. The famous Battle of Stirling Bridge was fought only a short distance from the castle's walls, and the fortress played a significant role in the Wars of Scottish Independence.

Later, the fortress was home to numerous Scottish kings and queens, including Mary Queen of Scots. The numerous installations and displays at the castle invite exploration and provide a window into Scotland's past while also bringing the history of the structure to life.

The Argyll and Sutherland Highlanders Regimental Museum, which recounts the history of one of Scotland's most illustrious military regiments, is another well-liked attraction at Stirling Castle. The museum showcases a broad variety of artifacts, including military gear and uniforms, weapons, and apparatus, as well as first-hand accounts from regimental members.

The city of Stirling, which also has a number of other sights and things to do, is where Stirling Castle is situated. The Wallace Monument and Church of the Holy Rude, which honor the life of Scottish hero William Wallace, are two of the city's many significant locations. The city is also home to a range of shops, restaurants, and galleries, as well as a bustling nightlife scene.

For anyone interested in Scotland's rich heritage and culture, Stirling Castle is a must-see location. The castle is a genuine gem of Scottish tourism with its magnificent architecture, intriguing exhibits and displays, and stunning position in the center of Stirling.

Another one of Scotland's most recognizable sites, Stirling Castle is situated in the center of the nation. As both a royal home and a fortress, the castle has been a significant part of Scottish history. The Great Hall, the Royal Palace, and the Castle Exhibition, which details the castle's extensive past, are just a few of the many attractions open to visitors.

The Royal Mile

The Palace of Holyroodhouse and Edinburgh Castle are located in the heart of Edinburgh's Old Town and are connected by the renowned Royal Mile. The Museum of Edinburgh and St. Giles' Church are just two of the historic buildings that line this street, which is a must-see for anyone interested in Scotland's rich history and culture.

The Royal Mile, in the heart of Edinburgh's Old Town, is a well-known thoroughfare that extends from Edinburgh Castle at the top of the hill all the way down to the Palace of Holyroodhouse at the bottom of the hill. This historic street, one of the most popular tourist sites in the city, is well known for its magnificent structures, rich past, and vivacious culture.

One of the most iconic features of the Royal Mile is its many historic buildings and landmarks. The street is lined with centuries-old buildings, including grand townhouses, elegant churches, and quaint shops and cafes.

Visitors can explore these buildings and learn about the many famous people and events that have shaped Scottish history, from the birthplace of economist Adam Smith to the site of the famous Covenanters' Prison.

Along with many other well-known landmarks and attractions, the Royal Mile is also the location of Saint Giles' Cathedral, a stunning Gothic building that has served as a place of worship for more than 900 years. The St. Giles' Throne and the Heart of Midlothian, a well-known stone heart that commemorates the location of the city's former prison, are just a few of the famous artworks and artifacts that can be found inside the cathedral.

The Scotch Whisky Experience, a distinctive museum and distillery that gives visitors the opportunity to learn about the history and culture of Scotland's most well-known beverage, is another well-liked destination on the Royal Mile. A visit of the distillery, tastings of various whiskies, and the opportunity to create your own whisky are all included in the experience.

A variety of stores, eateries, and cafes can be found along the Royal Mile, giving guests the opportunity to experience Scottish cuisine and culture. Visitors can taste regional specialties like haggis, neeps, and tatties as well as shop for trinkets and presents in the numerous boutiques and shops that line the street.

The renowned Edinburgh Fringe Festival, which takes place every August and features hundreds of shows and performances throughout the city, is one of many cultural events and festivals that take place on the Royal Mile throughout the year. The Edinburgh International Festival, the Royal Edinburgh Military Tattoo, and numerous others are additional activities.

Overall, anyone visiting Edinburgh should make sure to explore the Royal Mile. The street is a real gem of Scottish tourism with its stunning architecture, rich history and culture, and variety of attractions and activities.

Kelvingrove Art Center and Museum in Glasgow

In the center of Glasgow, the Kelvingrove Art Gallery and Museum is one of Scotland's most well-liked tourist destinations.

The museum is home to a sizable collection of artwork and artifacts, which includes pieces by many of Scotland's most well-known artists, as well as a variety of displays highlighting the history, culture, and natural heritage of the nation.

One of Glasgow's most cherished and recognizable landmarks is the Kelvingrove Art Gallery and Museum. The museum, which is located in the thriving West End neighborhood, is the repository of an amazing collection of works of art and artifacts that date back thousands of years in human history.

The Kelvingrove's stunning architecture is one of its most striking characteristics. In addition to making an impressive first impression, the museum's distinctive red sandstone facade and grand entry hall also give visitors a sense of the building's scale and grandeur through the size of its interior galleries and soaring ceilings.

Visitors can experience a variety of exhibits and collections inside the museum, ranging from modern art and design to artifacts from ancient Egypt.

The museum's art collection is especially noteworthy; it includes pieces by some of the most well-known painters in the world, such as Salvador Dali, Vincent Van Gogh, and Rembrandt.

The Kelvingrove's numerous interactive exhibits and displays, which breathe new and thrilling life into the museum's collections, are a noteworthy additional aspect. Visitors can walk inside a copy of a World War I trench to experience life for troops on the front lines or explore a recreated early 20th-century Glasgow street scene complete with stores, residences, and even a subway station.

The museum is also home to a range of family-friendly exhibits and activities, making it a great destination for visitors of all ages. Kids will love exploring the natural history galleries, which feature everything from dinosaurs to Scottish wildlife, while adults can immerse themselves in the museum's many art and design exhibits.

The West End neighborhood of Glasgow, which is home to the Kelvingrove, is also home to a number of other sights and entertainment options for tourists. Anyone visiting Glasgow should pay the neighborhood a visit because it offers everything from chic boutiques and hip cafés to important historical sites and a hopping nightlife.

In general, anyone interested in art, history, or culture should explore the Kelvingrove Art Gallery and Museum. The museum is a real gem of Scottish tourism with its stunning architecture, impressive collections, and variety of interactive displays and activities.

The Scottish Highlands

The Scottish Highlands are an area of breathtaking natural beauty, rugged terrain, and towering peaks. The famous Glencoe Valley, the charming town of Fort William, and the historic Culloden Battlefield are just a few of the many attractions in the area that tourists can experience.

The Scottish Highlands, a rocky and wild landscape of mountains, lochs, and forests that stretches across the northernmost portion of the nation, are one of Scotland's most breathtaking natural wonders.

The Highlands are a must-visit location for anyone visiting Scotland because of its untamed beauty, extensive past, and dynamic culture.

The numerous mountains and hills in the Scottish Highlands, including some of the highest peaks in the British Isles, are among the region's most recognizable characteristics. The Highlands provide countless chances for hiking, mountaineering, and other outdoor activities, from the imposing Ben Nevis to the majestic Cairngorms.

Numerous beautiful lochs, including the renowned Loch Ness, which is rumored to be the residence of the Loch Ness Monster, can also be found in the Highlands. Visitors can investigate the lochs' shorelines on foot or by boat while admiring the breathtaking views of the mountains and forests in the area.

The Scottish Highlands are also noteworthy for their extensive history and culture. Numerous historic places and landmarks, including ancient stone circles, medieval castles, and traditional Scottish villages, can be found in the region, which has been inhabited for many, many years. By visiting historical sites and museums, tourists can learn about the region's rich history. They can also get a taste of the local way of life by taking part in music, dance, and other traditional arts.

A variety of animals, including red deer, otters, eagles, and other local species, can be found in the Highlands. Visitors can take part in wildlife excursions, go on a bicycle or foot tour of the countryside, or simply experience the Highlands' natural beauty.

The Scottish Highlands also offer a variety of lodging choices, from comfortable bed and breakfasts to opulent hotels and cabins. Visitors have the option of staying in the region's quaint towns and villages or in the center of the countryside.

Ultimately, anyone visiting Scotland should make a point of visiting the Scottish Highlands. The Highlands are a true gem of Scottish tourism because of their breathtaking natural beauty, rich history and culture, and limitless possibilities for outdoor adventure.

The Cairngorms National Park

Another of Scotland's top tourist destinations, the Cairngorms National Park gives visitors the opportunity to explore some of the nation's most breathtaking landscapes.

In addition to hiking, mountain bicycling, and skiing in the winter, the park is home to a variety of wildlife, such as red deer, golden eagles, and mountain hares.

One of Scotland's most breathtaking natural marvels is the Cairngorms National Park, a vast area of craggy mountains, sweeping valleys, and old-growth forests that spans more than 4,500 square kilometers. The Cairngorms National Park is a must-see location for anyone visiting Scotland because of its exceptional natural beauty, diverse wildlife, and rich cultural history.

The Cairngorms National Park's numerous mountains and hills, which include some of the highest peaks in the British Isles, are among its most recognizable characteristics. Indulge in breath-taking views of the nearby landscapes and wildlife as you hike along one of the park's many hiking paths.

Some of the more difficult summits in the park, including Ben Macdui and Braeriach, are also accessible to mountaineers and climbers.

A wide array of wildlife, such as red deer, wildcats, pine martens, and various bird species, can be found in the Cairngorms National Park.

Visitors can take guided wildlife excursions to learn more about the area's abundant biodiversity or explore the park's numerous nature reserves and wildlife hotspots, such as the Glenmore Forest Park and the RSPB Abernethy reserve.

The rich cultural legacy of the Cairngorms National Park is another noteworthy aspect. Numerous historic places and landmarks, including ancient stone circles, medieval castles, and traditional Scottish villages, can be found in the region, which has been inhabited for many, many years. By visiting historical sites and museums, tourists can learn about the region's rich history. They can also get a taste of the local way of life by taking part in music, dance, and other traditional arts.

Outdoor adventure and recreation are also very common in the Cairngorms National Park. A variety of sports, such as skiing, snowboarding, mountain biking, kayaking, and more, are available to visitors. Numerous adventure sports businesses are based in the park and provide activities and guided trips for people of all ages and skill levels.

Last but not least, the Cairngorms National Park offers a variety of lodging choices, from inviting bed and breakfasts to opulent hotels and cabins. Visitors have the option of staying either in the park itself or in one of the quaint towns or villages that encircle it.

Overall, anyone visiting Scotland should make sure to explore the Cairngorms National Park. The park is a true gem of Scottish tourism because of its breathtaking natural beauty, varied wildlife, rich cultural heritage, and limitless opportunities for outdoor adventure.

In conclusion, tourists won't want to miss any of the many must-see sites in Scotland, a nation with a rich history, culture, and natural beauty.

Everyone can find something to enjoy in Scotland, from historic castles to breathtaking scenery. Make sure to put some of these top sites on your itinerary when making travel arrangements.

CHAPTER 3

Experiencing Scotland's Culture

Scotland's past and geography are deeply entwined with its rich and vibrant culture. Scotland's culture is a vital component of what makes the nation so distinctive and intriguing, from the traditional music and dance to the centuries-old customs and traditions.

Scotland's music is one of the best methods to experience its culture. Scottish traditional music is distinguished by its vivacious rhythms, eerie tunes, and use of instruments like the bagpipes, fiddles, and harps. Local pubs and bars often feature live traditional music, and visitors can also check out one of the many music events that take place all year long, like the Edinburgh International Festival or Glasgow's Celtic Connections Festival.

Literature is another significant component of Scottish society. With renowned authors like Sir Walter Scott, Robert Burns, and Irvine Welsh as natives, Scotland has a long and illustrious literary past.

By exploring historic libraries, bookshops, and museums, as well as by attending literary events and festivals like the Edinburgh International Book Festival, tourists can learn more about Scotland's literary heritage.

A rich cultural heritage with a long past can also be found in the Scottish Highlands. The Culloden Battlefield, the Loch Ness Monster Exhibition, and the Eilean Donan Castle are just a few of the numerous historical sites and notable locations in the area that tourists can experience. Visitors can also take part in customs and practices that are uniquely Scottish, such as the Highland Games, which are held annually and feature a variety of competitions, such as caber tossing, tug-of-war, and pipe band competitions.

Scottish cuisine has a rich history and is a significant part of the country's society. Haggis, neeps and tatties (mashed turnips and potatoes), Cullen skink (smoked haddock broth), and cullenbie are examples of traditional Scottish fare (a type of smoked fish). Visitors can partake in a traditional Scottish cooking class or taste these dishes and others at nearby eateries and bars.

Finally, getting to know the people of Scotland entails engaging in cultural experiences. Visitors can experience the warmth and friendliness that the Scots are known for by conversing with locals in pubs and eateries, going to local events and festivals, or even participating in a ceilidh (a traditional Scottish social event with music and dance).

Music and Sounds

Any trip to Scotland must include experiencing the local customs. Scotland's culture is a distinctive and fascinating fusion of the ancient and contemporary, and it is a true reflection of the history and heritage of the nation. This includes traditional music and literature as well as historical sites and customs. Visitors to Scotland can develop a better understanding of everything the country has to offer and forge enduring memories that will stick with them long after their trip is over by interacting with its people and traditions. Ballet and music Scotland's culture and traditions are deeply rooted in music and dance. Scottish traditional music is characterized by its vivacious rhythms, eerie tunes, and use of instruments like the bagpipes, fiddles, and harps. Dancing that is frequently performed to music is distinguished by vivacious footwork and complex routines.

The bagpipes, a wind instrument that has been played in Scotland for generations, are one of the most recognizable symbols of Scottish music. The sound of the bagpipes is frequently linked with military marches, and pipers playing at weddings, funerals, and other formal occasions are frequently seen donning traditional Scottish kilts.

The fiddle, a stringed instrument that has been performed in Scotland since the Middle Ages, is another prominent instrument in Scottish music. Traditional Scottish dance songs like reels and jigs, which have lively rhythms and intricate melodies, are frequently played on the fiddle.

Scotland not only has a flourishing traditional music scene but also a contemporary music culture with many talented musicians and bands. In recent years, indie rock, pop, and electronic music genres have grown in popularity, and many Scottish artists, including Annie Lennox, Calvin Harris, and Biffy Clyro, have found success abroad.

Scottish culture places a strong emphasis on dance, with a lengthy history of traditional dances like the ceilidh (pronounced kay-lee), a social dance in which groups of people circle dance.

The dances are frequently performed to live music at weddings, neighborhood gatherings, and celebrations.

Another well-liked dance style in Scotland is Scottish country dancing, which originated in the 18th century. The dance is frequently performed in formal settings, such as balls and dances, and it entails groups of couples performing a number of steps and movements to traditional Scottish music.

Overall, with a long past and a thriving modern scene, music and dance are significant components of Scottish culture. Visitors to Scotland can take part in a ceilidh or Scottish country dance event, visit music festivals and concerts, and experience local pub and bar music and dance. Visitors to Scotland can develop a better understanding of the culture of the nation and take home enduring memories by participating in the music and dance traditions of the country.

Scotland is renowned for its famous musical instrument makers, such as McCallum Bagpipes, who have been making handcrafted bagpipes since 1960, in addition to its traditional music and dance.

Visitors to Scotland are welcome to stop by these factories to observe the instrument-making process and to buy top-notch instruments to bring home as gifts.

Scotland is also home to a number of music and dance events, such as the Edinburgh International Festival, which presents a wide range of international musical, dance, and theatrical productions. The Edinburgh Military Tattoo, a renowned display of military bands and precision drill teams performed at Edinburgh Castle, is another highlight of the festival.

Visitors can enjoy Gaelic music from Scotland in addition to conventional Scottish music and dance. Gaelic music has its own distinctive sounds and rhythms. Gaelic music has been passed down through the generations, with traditional songs and melodies still being played today. Gaelic is an essential component of Scottish culture.

Visitors to Scotland can experience the distinctive vocal styles of Gaelic singing at Gaelic music performances and festivals, where they can hear the sounds of the traditional Gaelic harp, fiddle, and bagpipes.

Overall, Scotland's music and dance traditions are a vibrant and important part of the nation's culture, and tourists can fully immerse themselves in this rich heritage by going to performances and festivals, touring instrument makers, or even participating in a traditional Scottish ceilidh or country dance. Visitors can gain a deeper knowledge and appreciation of Scotland by participating in its musical and dance traditions.

Meals and beverages

Scottish cuisine has a rich history that encompasses both traditional and contemporary dishes. Scotland's culture is largely based on food and drink. As well as being known for its world-famous whiskey and beer, Scotland is renowned for its premium native foods like beef, game, and seafood.

The savory pudding known as haggis, which is prepared from sheep's offal, onions, oats, and spices, is among the most well-known traditional Scottish foods. It is a standard dish at Burns Suppers, a celebration of the life and works of Scottish poet Robert Burns celebrated on his birthday, January 25, and is frequently served with "neeps and tatties," or mashed turnips and potatoes.

Other well-known Scottish dishes include cullen skink, a rich soup made from smoked haddock, and Cullen beef, a cut of beef from the northeastern Scottish town of Cullen that is prized for its taste and tenderness. With many Scottish rivers offering some of the finest salmon fishing in the world, Scottish salmon is also highly prized.

Scotland is known for its traditional cuisine, as well as its vibrant modern food scene, which features many talented chefs and restaurants serving up creative and interesting food. Particularly in Edinburgh, Michelin-starred eateries that highlight Scottish ingredients in unique and imaginative ways include The Kitchin and Restaurant Martin Wishart.

With numerous famed distilleries spread out across the nation, Scotland is perhaps best known for its whisky when it comes to alcoholic beverages. Visitors to Scotland have the opportunity to partake in distillery visits where they can learn about the production of whisky and taste some of the finest single malts in the world.

Scotland's craft beer industry is flourishing, with numerous tiny breweries creating distinctive, flavorful beers using regional ingredients.

Craft beer has seen a rise in popularity in recent years, with many beer connoisseurs searching out novel and intriguing brews.

BrewDog, which is well-known throughout the world for its inventive and experimental beers, and Tempest Brewing Co., which focuses on using regional Scottish ingredients in its beers, are two of the most well-known Scottish artisan breweries. Other noteworthy breweries include Harviestoun Brewery, which creates a variety of award-winning beers, including the well-known Old Engine Oil, and Fyne Ales, which is situated in the picturesque Loch Lomond and Trossachs National Park.

Scotland is also the location of numerous beer events, such as the well-known Edinburgh Craft Beer Festival and the Great Scottish Beer Celebration in Glasgow, where guests can taste a wide variety of Scottish and foreign beers. The best Scottish craft beer can be found at these festivals, which are also a wonderful place to meet other beer lovers.

Many Scottish breweries are experimenting with new flavors and styles in addition to traditional Scotch ales, including sour beers, IPAs, and stouts.

Visitors can experience the variety and creativity of Scotland's beer scene and develop a greater understanding of the nation's brewing customs by sampling various beers from Scottish craft breweries.

Scotland has a long culinary history that is reflected in its geography and events. The nation is renowned for its robust and flavorful food, which frequently incorporates locally sourced ingredients like game, seafood, and root veggies. Cullen skink, cullenary, neeps and tatties, haggis, and neeps and tatties are some of Scotland's most well-known foods.

The dish known as haggis, which is typically wrapped in a sheep's stomach, is made from minced sheep heart, liver, and lungs along with onion, oatmeal, and spices. Any visitor to Scotland must taste it; it is typically served with neeps and tatties (mashed turnips and potatoes). Cullenary is a variety of smoked haddock, and cullen skink is a thick soup prepared with smoked haddock, potatoes, and onions.

Scotland is also home to a large number of top-notch seafood eateries, especially in seaside cities like Oban and St. Andrews.

Visitors can taste local specialties like smoked salmon as well as fresh Scottish seafood like lobster, langoustines, and scallops. Along with its seafood, Scotland is renowned for its top-notch beef and game, including pheasant and venison, both of which can be found on many eatery menus.

Scotland is renowned for its whisky, a beverage produced from malted barley, water, and oak barrel aging. Visitors can tour Scotland's whisky distilleries and taste the various whiskies made in the country's various regions, including Islay, Speyside, and the Highlands. The most well-known Scotch whiskey are Talisker, Macallan, and Glenlivet.

Scotland makes a variety of alcoholic beverages in addition to whisky, including gin, beer, and cider. Scottish gin has become more well-known recently, thanks to the numerous small producers that use regional botanicals to create distinctive and flavorful gins. Many small breweries in Scotland are creating distinctive and experimental beers, and the country's craft beer is developing a reputation for quality and innovation.

There is something for every taste and budget in Scotland's food and drink scene, which is a rich and varied reflection of its culture and past. Visitors can taste traditional Scottish fare and beverages and learn more about the nation's expanding craft food and beverage scene.

Shopping and Crafts

Many towns and cities in Scotland offer a variety of stores and markets that highlight regional goods and crafts, and the country is well-known for its thriving retail scene and rich craft traditions.

Edinburgh, which has a variety of boutique shops, high-end fashion stores, and independent merchants, is one of the most well-liked locations in Scotland for shopping. In addition to specialty shops selling regionally produced crafts and gifts, the historic Royal Mile is lined with shops offering Scottish tartan, kilts, and other traditional clothing. Princes Street and George Street, two additional well-liked shopping districts in Edinburgh, provide a variety of high-end clothing and luxury products.

Visitors can tour Glasgow's bustling Merchant City neighborhood, which is renowned for its independent boutiques and artisan stores. Glasgow's West End is another well-liked retail area, with a variety of retro and vintage stores, as well as book and record shops.

Scotland also has a large number of craft fairs and markets where tourists can peruse and buy locally made crafts and goods. The Edinburgh Farmers Market, which sells a variety of fresh produce and artisanal goods, and the Glasgow Christmas Market, which offers a variety of crafts and gifts from local artists and designers, are two of the most well-liked markets.

Tartan, a patterned fabric that is historically connected with Scottish Highland dress, is one of the most recognizable examples of Scottish craftsmanship. At the National Museum of Scotland in Edinburgh, visitors can investigate the tartan's past and discover more about other traditional Scottish arts and crafts like weaving, ceramics, and glassblowing.

Scotland is home to an increasing number of contemporary designers and artists, many of whom are creating inventive and modern designs that are inspired by Scotland's heritage and landscape in addition to traditional crafts. Independent shops and galleries throughout Scotland as well as occasions like the Edinburgh Art Festival and the Glasgow International Festival of Visual Art are places where visitors can view the creations of these designers and artists.

Scotland's shopping and craft scene, in general, offers a distinctive and varied reflection of the nation's culture and history and is a must-see for any tourist interested in discovering the best of Scottish creativity and design.

Visitors to Scotland can take part in a variety of interactive workshops and classes where they can learn about traditional Scottish crafts and methods in addition to shopping and window-shopping.

A common choice is to enroll in a weaving or spinning lesson, which are offered all over Scotland. Visitors can learn about Scottish textile heritage and practice weaving or spinning their own fabric or yarn. Additionally, there are pottery classes where guests can create their own piece of clay pottery while learning about the lengthy past of Scottish pottery.

Through workshops and demonstrations, visitors can also learn about traditional Scottish music and dance. The bagpipes are one of the most recognizable Scottish instruments, and Scottish traditional music is recognized for its upbeat and repetitive style. Visitors can take in local musicians' concerts and acts or even enroll in bagpipe lessons to learn how to play this age-old instrument.

Another well-liked pastime is Scottish traditional dance, with ceilidhs (pronounced kay-lees) being a type of Scottish social event where dancing and live music are performed. To learn traditional Scottish dances like the Highland Fling, the Sword Dance, or the Scottish Country Dance, visitors can join a ceilidh or enroll in a dance workshop.

Overall, visitors can enjoy a wide variety of activities, from music and dance to shopping and crafts, thanks to Scotland's culture and customs. There is something for everyone to find and appreciate in Scotland, whether you're interested in modern interpretations of Scottish creativity or traditional techniques.

CHAPTER 4

Exploring Scotland's Natural Beauty

Scotland is renowned for its stunning natural beauty, which is a key reason why many people choose to visit this small yet diverse country. From rugged coastlines and sweeping glens to misty mountains and peaceful lochs, there are plenty of ways to explore Scotland's natural wonders.

Walking or hiking are two of the most well-liked methods to take in Scotland's natural beauty. There are lots of trails and paths in the nation, from short strolls to strenuous multi-day treks. The John Muir Way, the Great Glen Way, and the West Highland Way are a few of the most recognizable trekking trails. These paths all provide distinctive scenery and difficulties, and they're all wonderful opportunities to get up close and personal with Scotland's breathtaking landscapes.

Driving is another well-liked method of taking in Scotland's natural splendor. There are many scenic routes in the nation, such as the Scottish Borders Route, which leads travelers through charming towns, important historical sites, and breathtaking natural settings, and the North Coast 500, a 500-mile loop around Scotland's northern shore.

Scotland's natural grandeur can also be discovered by boat by visitors. Numerous lochs and rivers are well-liked for boating, fishing, and just taking in the peaceful majesty of the Scottish countryside. For instance, the renowned Loch Ness is well-known for its breathtaking natural scenery and calm waters in addition to its legendary monster.

Scotland is also home to a variety of outdoor sports and activities, including kayaking, mountain biking, rock climbing, and skiing, for those who prefer an adrenaline-fueled experience. Hiking, skiing, and snowboarding are just a few of the outdoor pursuits and sports available to tourists in the Cairngorms National Park.

One of Scotland's biggest assets is its pristine environment, which presents a plethora of opportunities for exploration and adventure. There are many ways to explore and enjoy Scotland's diverse and beautiful landscapes, from hiking and walking to driving and water activities.

Scotland's natural grandeur extends beyond its glens, lochs, and mountains. A variety of animals, including red deer, otters, seals, dolphins, and various bird species, can be found throughout the nation.

Many tourists travel to Scotland expressly to view the local wildlife, whether they do so by going on a wildlife tour, going to a nature preserve, or just keeping an eye out while driving through the countryside.

Scotland is renowned for having beautiful coastlines, many of which are tucked away in outlying regions. Scotland's beaches give tourists a variety of scenery and experiences, from the white sands of the Outer Hebrides to the rocky shores of the north coast.

Luskentyre on the Isle of Harris, Achmelvich in the northwest Highlands, and Saint Andrews in Fife are a few of the most well-known beaches.

Scotland's cultural and historical heritage are tightly entwined with its natural beauty. The ruins of castles and abbeys that are tucked away in the hills and valleys are just one example of the stunning natural settings where many of the nation's historical sites and landmarks can be found.

One illustration is the abandoned castle of Dunnottar, which is perched atop a rocky outcropping on Scotland's east coast and offers breathtaking views of the North Sea.

A visit to one of Scotland's many gardens or parks is another opportunity to take in the country's natural beauty. Scotland is home to a variety of public and private gardens, from the private grounds at Balmoral Castle to the Royal Botanic Garden in Edinburgh. Each of these gardens provides chances to learn about Scotland's horticultural history and traditions in addition to its own distinctive plant life and landscapes.

In general, Scotland's beautiful natural surroundings play a big role in why so many tourists decide to travel there. Scotland provides a wealth of chances to discover and enjoy its varied and breathtaking landscapes, whether you're interested in hiking and walking, water sports, wildlife, beaches, historic sites, or gardens.

Hiking and Walking

In Scotland, exploring the country's mountains, hills, and coastal paths by walking or hiking is a very common activity.

The Scottish countryside provides a variety of hiking and strolling opportunities, ranging from easy strolls through gardens and woodlands to more difficult hikes up steep mountains.

The West Highland Way, a 154-kilometer path that connects Milngavie, a small town outside Glasgow, with Fort William in the Scottish Highlands, is one of the most well-known hiking routes in Scotland. The path travels through a variety of breathtaking landscapes, such as the Rannoch Moor wilderness, the banks of Loch Lomond, and the striking Glencoe mountains. For hikers, the West Highland Way is a well-liked option, with both guided and self-guided excursions available.

The Isle of Skye is another well-liked location for hiking and has a variety of paths for hikers of all experience levels. For instance, the Old Man of Storr is a brief but steep trek that rewards visitors with breathtaking views of the island's coastline, while the Quiraing is a moderately difficult hike that leads visitors through a series of unusual rock formations.

There are many forests and parks in Scotland that provide calm walks and easy hikes for those seeking a more relaxed hiking experience. For those who enjoy hiking and plants, the Royal Botanic Garden in Edinburgh is a popular option, and the Falls of Bruar in Perthshire offer a peaceful stroll through a lovely wooded gorge.

For hikers and walkers, Scotland's breathtaking landscapes and diverse terrain provide a wealth of possibilities. Scotland's hiking and walking trails are guaranteed to motivate and challenge visitors of all ages and abilities, offering everything from strenuous mountain climbs to leisurely woodland strolls.

Scotland has a number of other hiking locations worth visiting in addition to the West Highland Way and the Isle of Skye. For instance, the Cairngorms National Park, the biggest national park in the UK, has a variety of hiking paths that wind through woodlands, over mountain passes, and across moorland that is covered in heather.

Another well-liked hiking location is the Glencoe region, which is renowned for its breathtaking scenery and dramatic peaks.

The Devil's Staircase is a strenuous trek that offers expansive views of the surrounding mountains, and the Buachaille Etive Mor, a distinctive peak with a pyramidal shape, is a favorite among hikers.

Scotland offers a number of beautiful trails that wind along its rocky coastline for those who enjoy coastal strolls. For instance, the 117-kilometer-long Fife Coastal Path passes by fishing communities, beaches, and historical places as it travels from the Firth of Forth to the Firth of Tay. Another well-known coastal path is the 215-kilometer John Muir Way, which connects Dunbar on the east coast to Helensburgh on the west coast.

It's crucial to pack the right apparel and equipment for a hike in Scotland because the weather can change suddenly and abruptly. Even on sunny days, a decent set of hiking boots, a waterproof jacket and pair of pants, and warm layers are necessities.

The country's natural beauty can be experienced up close and personal on Scotland's hiking and walking paths, regardless of whether you are an expert hiker or a beginner.

There is a hike in Scotland for every skill level, with choices varying from leisurely strolls to strenuous mountain climbs.

Wildlife and Nature

The breathtaking natural beauty and varied wildlife of Scotland are well known. Scotland's landscapes are home to a broad variety of creatures that can be seen in their natural habitats, from majestic deer to playful otters.

The Cairngorms National Park, which is home to several deer species, including red deer, Roe deer, and Sika deer, is one of the best locations to observe Scotland's wildlife. Along with pine martens, foxes, and badgers, the forest is also home to the elusive Scottish wildcat, one of the rarest cats in the world.

Another popular destination for wildlife lovers is the Isle of Skye, where visitors can observe sea eagles, puffins, seals, and even whales and dolphins from the island's rugged shoreline. Red deer can frequently be seen grazing on the slopes of the island, which is also where they are found in large numbers.

Seals, dolphins, and whales are just a few of the marine animals that call Scotland's seas home. There is a good possibility of seeing bottlenose dolphins, seals, and porpoises in the Moray Firth, which is off the east coast of Scotland.

A wide range of vegetation and fauna can be found in Scotland's natural landscapes, including ancient woodlands, meadows covered in wildflowers, and moorland covered in heather.

Some of the most well-known species in the UK can be found in the Scottish Highlands, including the rare and historic Caledonian pine forest, which is home to red squirrels, pine martens, and capercaillie, a variety of grouse.

Scotland offers a wealth of chances to experience its diverse wildlife and natural beauty up close, whether you're a serious wildlife enthusiast or you just like to spend time in nature. There are numerous opportunities to experience Scotland's wildlife and landscapes, including guided excursions, wildlife safaris, and nature walks.

In addition to offering many chances for outdoor pursuits like hiking, fishing, and birdwatching, Scotland's natural beauty also offers.

Both experienced hikers and casual walkers have the opportunity to explore the nation's breathtaking landscapes thanks to the extensive network of hiking paths that it has to offer.

The West Highland Way is one of the most well-known hiking routes in Scotland. It is 96 miles long and brings hikers from Milngavie, a small town outside of Glasgow, to Fort William while passing through the untamed areas of Loch Lomond, Rannoch Moor, and Glencoe.

With numerous opportunities for rest stops along the route, the trail can be finished in six to eight days.

In Scotland, fishing is another well-liked outdoor pastime. There are many rivers and lochs where you can go trout and salmon fishing. One of the most well-known fishing rivers in the nation is the River Tweed, which flows through the Scottish Borders. The River Spey, located in the heart of the Scottish Highlands, is famed for its salmon fishing.

Scotland offers excellent opportunities for birdwatching, including the opportunity to see puffins, ospreys, and golden eagles.

Birdwatchers flock to the Isle of Mull, which is off the shore of Scotland, to see sea eagles, puffins, and other seabirds in their natural settings.

The many museums, castles, and historic sites in Scotland allow visitors to learn more about the country's lengthy and fascinating past in addition to its natural beauty. Scotland extends a warm welcome to visitors from all over the world, regardless of whether their interests are in experiencing the country's natural landscapes, its culture and history, or simply in enjoying its cuisine, beverages, and hospitality.

Water Activities

Scotland is a well-liked location for those looking for water-based adventure because of its extensive coastline and inland waterways. There are many opportunities to experience Scotland's waterways, from sailing and fishing to kayaking and paddleboarding.

Kayaking is one of the most famous water sports in Scotland, where there are lochs, rivers, and a breathtaking coastline to paddle along.

Scotland's west coast is an especially popular location for sea kayaking because it offers the chance to paddle around islands and discover secluded coves and sea caves. For instance, the Isle of Skye provides a variety of kayaking excursions, from easy paddles along protected bays to more difficult sea kayaking expeditions.

Another well-liked activity in Scotland is paddleboarding, which allows for leisurely exploration of the country's numerous lochs and waterways. Paddleboarding is very popular on Loch Lomond, Scotland's biggest inland waterway, where you can enjoy the beautiful mountain scenery while paddling along its calm waters.

Scotland offers the chance to charter a yacht or take part in a sailing excursion to experience the stunning coastline of the nation. Scotland's west coast is especially well-known for sailing due to the numerous islands and sheltered bays that make for the perfect sailing experience.

Scotland's rivers and lochs provide some of the best salmon and trout fishing in the entire globe for anglers.

There are many places to cast a line and attempt your luck at catching a fish, from the River Tweed in the Scottish Borders to the River Spey in the Highlands.

Scotland's waterways also provide chances for swimming, diving, and even surfing in addition to these activities. Some of the finest surfing spots in the nation are on Scotland's north coast, where both novice and expert surfers can enjoy the waves.

Overall, whether you're looking to paddle, sail, fish, or simply take a dip in its clear waters, Scotland's waterways offer a wealth of opportunities for adventure and discovery. For anyone who enjoys the great outdoors, Scotland is a must-visit location because of its breathtaking scenery and friendly people.

Scotland's waterways provide a singular viewpoint of the nation's natural grandeur and a chance to get up close and personal with some of its most famous wildlife, such as seals, dolphins, and even whales.

Some of the most isolated and stunning coastlines in the world, with rocky peaks and unspoiled beaches, can be found on the Scottish islands, such as the Inner and Outer Hebrides. Taking a wildlife-watching boat trip is a well-liked exercise where you can see whales, dolphins, and porpoises in addition to a variety of seabirds like puffins, gannets, and razorbills.

Scotland's numerous inland lochs offer a tranquil environment for paddling, kayaking, or paddleboarding. The most well-known loch in the nation, Loch Ness, is also one of the deepest and is a favorite destination for tourists because it is thought to be the home of a mysterious monster. However, there are numerous other stunning lochs to discover, including Lake Lomond, Loch Awe, and Loch Tay.

Scotland also provides white-water rafting chances on rivers like the River Tay and River Findhorn for those who want to feel the rush of the rapids. With breathtaking views of the surroundings, these swiftly moving rivers offer the ideal backdrop for an exhilarating adventure.

Sea kayakers have a ton of chances to explore rocky coves and remote beaches along Scotland's coastline. The Isle of Skye is one of the most well-liked sea kayaking locations, where you can paddle around the island's rugged shoreline while admiring the Cuillin Mountains.

Scotland's waterways have something to offer everyone, whether you're a seasoned water-sports enthusiast or a beginner looking to attempt something new. Scotland's waterways are the ideal location for an unforgettable outdoor experience thanks to its untamed and rugged coastline, serene lochs, and plentiful wildlife.

Conclusion

In summation, Scotland is a place where everyone can find something to enjoy. Scotland is a place that everyone should visit because of its fascinating past, vibrant culture, and stunning natural beauty. Scotland has something to offer every traveler, whether they want to experience the country's ancient castles, indulge in its delectable food, or immerse themselves in its thriving arts and music scene.

Scotland will win your heart and leave you with lifelong memories thanks to its amiable residents, warm ambiance, and breathtaking landscapes. So why not plan your trip right away and take advantage of everything that amazing nation has to offer?

We sincerely hope that this guide has given you all the details you need to organize the ideal Scottish journey, and we can't wait to welcome you to our stunning nation.

Scotland is a special and unforgettable location due to its rich history and culture as well as its breathtaking landscapes.

Scotland offers something for everyone, whether you want to visit its Wander through its wild mountains, visit its bustling towns, or enjoy its folk music and performance.

Scotland's history and culture are so ingrained in daily living, which is one of its most amazing characteristics. Scotland's cultural customs are still very much in existence today, from the Highland Games to traditional ceilidhs. Attending one of the many fairs or events that are held throughout the year allows visitors to Scotland to do just that.

Scotland is a nation that is also enthusiastic about its cuisine and beverages. Scotland's cuisine is a mirror of its varied landscapes and distinctive cultural legacy, and features ingredients like fresh seafood, locally sourced produce, and world-famous Scotch whisky. Visitors can taste the many different kinds of whisky made in the nation's numerous distilleries, as well as everything from traditional haggis and neeps to modern fusion cuisine.

Scotland is a nation known for its natural beauty in addition to its culture and food.

Scotland's natural environments are absolutely breathtaking, from the rough terrain of the Scottish Highlands to the serene beauty of the nation's numerous lochs. Visitors can get up close and personal with some of the nation's most famous animals, such as seals, dolphins, and eagles, while exploring this beauty on foot, bicycle, or even by boat.

Generally, anyone who travels to Scotland will have a positive experience. Scotland is a place that everyone should visit because of its fascinating history and culture, breathtaking natural scenery, and hospitable people.

Made in the USA
Middletown, DE
20 November 2023